Copyright © Jonathan Lee 2005

Published 2005 by CWR, Waverley Abbey House, Waverley Lane, Farnham, Surrey GU9 8EP, England.

The right of Jonathan Lee to be identified as the author and illustrator of this work has been asserted by him in accordance with the Copyright, Designs and Patents Act 1988.

All rights reserved. No part of this publication may be reproduced, stored in a retrieval system, or transmitted, in any form or by any means, electronic, mechanical, photocopying, recording or otherwise, without the prior permission in writing of CWR.

See back of book for list of National Distributors.

Bible verses taken from the Good News Bible copyright © American Bible Society 1966, 1971, 1976, 1992, 1994.

Concept development, editing, design and production by CWR.

Illustrations: Jonathan Lee

Printed in England by Linney Print

ISBN 1-85345-363-3

Remember When Jesus Healed The Sick

Written and illustrated by Jonathan Lee

It was spring outside and the school gardens were full of flowers. The children, as always, were looking forward to hearing what Mrs Phips had to read them at the end of the school day. With the class on the reading carpet, Mrs Phips cleared her throat, 'Uh hem,' and began to read . . .

A big crowd of people had gathered on the shore of Capernaum to wait for Jesus as he arrived by boat. They had heard of His wonderful miracles and teaching, but before anyone had the chance to say anything, running through the crowd came a man called Jairus, a leader of the synagogue.

As he came to Jesus he fell on his knees before Him and said, 'My little daughter lies sick at home and is dying. Please come and touch her so that she may be healed and live.' Without delay Jesus went with him as the ever-growing crowd pushed and shoved to be near Jesus . . .

Among the crowd was a poor woman who had been ill for twelve years. She had been to many doctors, but no one could help her.

She thought to herself if she could only touch the hem of Jesus' clothing she would be healed.

As she pushed her way though the crowd with all her might she tried to reach Jesus.

With one final effort she reached out...

She told Jesus how she had suffered for twelve years. Jesus said to her, 'Daughter, your faith has made you well; go in peace and be free of your illness.' And from that moment, she was well and lived every day in that peace.

Whilst this was happening a man from Jairus' house came to him and said, 'Your daughter has died, don't bother Jesus anymore.'

When Jesus heard this He said, 'Don't be afraid, just believe.' Jesus took Peter, James and John with Him and set off for Jairus' house...

When they arrived they could see that everyone was very upset.
'Why is everyone crying?' asked Jesus.
'This little girl is not dead. She is just sleeping.'

The people laughed at Jesus for saying that she was asleep, so He sent them away and went into the little girl's room with her parents and His disciples. Jairus and his wife had tried everything to make their only daughter get better.

She was lying so peaceful and still as Jesus went over to her bedside . . .

She looked very pale and thin as she had not eaten for so long. Jesus took her frail hand and said, 'Little girl, get up.'

Immediately she opened her eyes, sat up and even **began** to walk around the room. She was about twelve years old.

The class had never heard such a remarkable story before. From the hushed amazement a little boy called Richard put his hand up and asked...

'Mrs Phips, can Jesus still heal people today, because so many are sick and unwell?' It was a very good question and Mrs Phips had to think carefully about her answer . . .

We may know people close to us who aren't well. We may even know people who have died despite our prayers. But never forget, Jesus still can and does heal people today in miraculous ways.

He is always there for each one of us, so no matter what happens or how sad a situation may be ...

Remember when Jesu...

Revelation Ch. 21 v. 4 → fill in the missing **letters** to find out what God has promised He will do one day...

v4 'He will **wipe** away all **tears** from their **eyes**. There will be **no more** death, no more **grief** or **crying** or **pain**. The **old** things have **disappeared**.'

MEMORY VERSE
Jesus says... 'Do not be worried and upset'. John Ch. 14 v 1

Colour In Pages

National Distributors

UK: (and countries not listed below)
CWR, Waverley Abbey House, Waverley Lane, Farnham, Surrey GU9 8EP.
Tel: (01252) 784700 Outside UK +44 (0)1252 784700

AUSTRALIA: CMC Australasia, PO Box 519, Belmont, Victoria 3216.
Tel: (03) 5241 3288

CANADA: Cook Communications Ministries, PO Box 98, 55 Woodslee Avenue, Paris, Ontario.
Tel: 1800 263 2664

GHANA: Challenge Enterprises of Ghana, PO Box 5723, Accra.
Tel: (021) 222437/223249 Fax: (021) 226227

HONG KONG: Cross Communications Ltd, 1/F, 562A Nathan Road, Kowloon.
Tel: 2780 1188 Fax: 2770 6229

INDIA: Crystal Communications, 10-3-18/4/1, East Marredpalli, Secunderabad – 500026. Andhra Pradesh, Tel/Fax: (040) 27737145

KENYA: Keswick Books and Gifts Ltd, PO Box 10242, Nairobi.
Tel: (02) 331692/226047 Fax: (02) 728557

MALAYSIA: Salvation Book Centre (M) Sdn Bhd, 23 Jalan SS 2/64, 47300 Petaling Jaya, Selangor.
Tel: (03) 78766411/78766797 Fax: (03) 78757066/78756360

NEW ZEALAND: CMC Australasia, PO Box 36015, Lower Hutt.
Tel: 0800 449 408 Fax: 0800 449 049

NIGERIA: FBFM, Helen Baugh House, 96 St Finbarr's College Road, Akoka, Lagos.
Tel: (01) 7747429/4700218/825775/827264

PHILIPPINES: OMF Literature Inc, 776 Boni Avenue, Mandaluyong City.
Tel: (02) 531 2183 Fax: (02) 531 1960

REPUBLIC OF IRELAND: Scripture Union, 40 Talbot Street, Dublin 1.
Tel: (01) 8363764

SINGAPORE: Armour Publishing Pte Ltd, Block 203A Henderson Road, 11–06 Henderson Industrial Park, Singapore 159546.
Tel: 6 276 9976 Fax: 6 276 7564

SOUTH AFRICA: Struik Christian Books, 80 MacKenzie Street, PO Box 1144, Cape Town 8000.
Tel: (021) 462 4360 Fax: (021) 461 3612

SRI LANKA: Christombu Books, 27 Hospital Street, Colombo 1.
Tel: (01) 433142/328909

TANZANIA: CLC Christian Book Centre, PO Box 1384, Mkwepu Street, Dar es Salaam.
Tel/Fax (022) 2119439

USA: Cook Communications Ministries, PO Box 98, 55 Woodslee Avenue, Paris, Ontario, Canada.
Tel: 1800 263 2664

ZIMBABWE: Word of Life Books, Shop 4, Memorial Building, 35 S Machel Avenue, Harare.
Tel: (04) 781305 Fax: (04) 774739

For email addresses, visit the CWR website: www.cwr.org.uk

CWR is a registered charity – number 294387

Titles in this series

Remember The Wise and Foolish Builders
ISBN: 1-85345-303-X

Remember The Good Samaritan
ISBN: 1-85345-301-3

Remember The Lost Sheep
ISBN: 1-85345-302-1

Remember When Jesus Walked on the Sea
ISBN: 1-85345-362-5

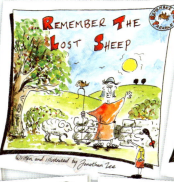
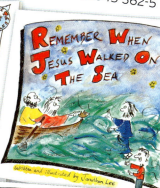

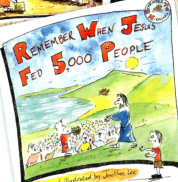

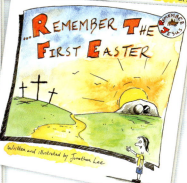

Remember When Jesus Fed 5000 People
ISBN: 1-85345-361-7

Remember The First Christmas
ISBN: 1-85345-317-X

Remember The First Easter
ISBN: 1-85345-330-7

All books **£3.99** each (plus p&p)

Prices correct at time of printing